The Camp System

Jane Shuter

Heinemann Library
Chicago, Illinois

Design by Joanna Sapwell and Tinstar Design
Illustrations by Martin Griffin
Originated by Ambassador Litho Ltd
Printed in Hong Kong, by Wing King Tong

07 06 05 04 03
10 9 8 7 6 5 4 3 2 1

**Library of Congress
Cataloging-in-Publication Data**
Shuter, Jane.
  The camp system / Jane Shuter.
    v. cm. -- (The Holocaust)
Includes bibliographical references and index.
Contents: Types of camps -- Types of prisoners -- How
camps were used -- Running the camps -- Camp discipline
-- Efficient camps -- Processing arrivals -- List of camps.
  ISBN 1-4034-0809-2 (HC), 1-4034-3201-5 (Pbk.)
  1. Holocaust, Jewish (1939-1945)--Juvenile literature. 2.
World War, 1939-1945--Concentration camps--Juvenile
literature. [1. Holocaust, Jewish (1939-1945) 2.
Concentration camps.] I. Title. II. Holocaust
(Chicago, Ill.)
  D804.34 .S635 2002
  940.53'18--dc21
                            2002006754

Acknowledgments
The author and publishers are grateful to the following for
permission to reproduce copyright material: pp. 4, 13, 26,
42 AKG; p. 5 Popperfoto; p. 6 Weimar Picture Library; p. 7
Yad Vashem; pp. 9, 10, 11, 12, 38, 46, 47, 49 USHMM; pp.
14, 18 Tomi Ungerer & Diogene Verlag AG Zurich; p. 15
Ullstein Bilder Dienst; pp. 16, 25, 27, 36, 43, 44
Auschwitz-Birkenau State Museum; p. 17 Corbis; p. 19 The
Good Old Days; p. 20 BPK; pp. 22, 31, 33, 40 Auschwitz
Museum; pp. 24, 24, 28, 32, 34, 37, 45 Emma Robertson &
Magnet Harlequin; p. 29 Mary Evans Picture Library; p. 35
Ullstein Bild; p. 39 Emma Robertson.

Cover photograph shows camp records of prisoners at
Auschwitz, reproduced with permission of USHMM.

Special thanks to Ronald Smelser and Sally Brown-Winter.

About the series consultants
Ronald Smelser is a history professor at the University
of Utah. He has written or edited eight books on the
Holocaust and over three dozen articles. His recent
publications include *Learning About the Holocaust: A Student
Guide* (4 vol.) and *Lessons and Legacies: The Holocaust and
Justice*. Professor Smelser is also a past president of the
German Studies Association.

Sally Brown-Winter has worked in the field of Jewish
Education as a principal and teacher for over 25 years.
In her schools, the Shoah—its history, lessons, and
implications—have been explored from kindergarten
through high school.

Every effort has been made to contact copyright holders of
any material reproduced in this book. Any omissions will
be rectified in subsequent printings if notice is given to
the publisher.

Some words are shown in bold, **like this.** You can find out what they mean by looking
in the glossary.

Contents

Camps and the Holocaust

When the **Nazi** Party, led by Adolf Hitler, came to power in Germany in 1933, it wanted to set up the perfect Nazi state. The Nazis wanted to stamp out any opposition to their rule, so they set up a system of camps for holding people they saw as **"undesirable."** The Nazis said the camps would re-educate prisoners to accept Nazi ideas. Camps were different from ordinary prisons because the prisoners had not been convicted of any crime and there was no date set for their release.

The early camps were **concentration camps** for **political** opponents. The first of these, Dachau, was set up just a few days after the Nazis won the March 1933 election.

The camps were run by the **SS** (short for *Schutzstaffel*, or "security staff"). The SS had been set up as Hitler's private bodyguard, and they all swore an oath of loyalty to Hitler, not Germany. Led by Heinrich Himmler, the SS grew to become a powerful empire within Nazi Germany.

Early Prisoners

Some of the earliest prisoners in Dachau concentration camp were political opponents of the Nazis, mostly **Communists** and Social Democrats, like the prisoners in this photograph.

Some were **Jewish,** but they were there for their political beliefs, not what the Nazis saw as their **race.** The camp was built to hold 5,000 people. The rules read to prisoners arriving in Dachau began:

Tolerance means weakness. Punishment will be mercilessly handed out whenever Germany's interests make it necessary. A person who is decent but misled will never be affected by these punishment regulations. But political stirrers be warned: watch out that you are not caught, for you will be hung.

Different Prisoners

Before long, the Nazis were using the camps not only to hold political opponents, but also to imprison all kinds of people that they did not want in their perfect state. Among these were Jews. Jews see themselves as a people with common ancestors who can be traced back to Biblical times. Jews are united by their religion—Judaism—and by a strong culture. The Nazis also called people Jews if they had Jewish ancestors, even if they had changed their faith. The Nazis eventually moved from imprisoning Jews to killing all Jews in German-controlled lands. This mass murder of about six million Jews, and other so-called undesirables, is called the **Holocaust.** The camps were vital in making the Holocaust happen.

How Were Ghettos Different from Camps?

Ghettos were areas of towns walled off from the rest of the town. Jews were forced to live in ghettos. They were crowded, but families could live together and follow their religion. In a camp, families were split up. All prisoners had to follow prison routine, from morning to night. There were regular **roll calls** so guards could be sure everyone was there. Camp prisoners ate only camp food and did the work the guards gave them. They could not follow their religion. This book only looks at the camps and the way they were run. Another book in this series, *Life and Death in Hitler's Europe,* will look more closely at life in the ghettos.

How Do We Know?

- One of the most important sources of information are survivors of the camps. Some told their memories directly, others wrote stories and poems, or painted and drew the camps.
- Official Nazi documents show what went on in the camps, although the Nazis did try to destroy the evidence.
- A few camps, such as Dachau and Auschwitz-Birkenau, still stand.
- The Nuremberg Trials of 1945 and 1946, held after the defeat of Germany in World War II, used descriptions of what went on in the camps.
- Some people who did not survive hid writings or pictures that were later found.
- The soldiers who **liberated** the camps recorded what they saw in words, on film, and in pictures.

Types of Camps

There were three main types of camps: **concentration camps, labor camps,** and **death camps.** They were the same in that:

- They were fenced off from the outside world, guarded, and run by soldiers.
- They gave prisoners the bare minimum of food and shelter.
- People were imprisoned there without trial and were given no date for their release. They were badly treated and harshly punished.
- The biggest camps had at least one **crematorium** for burning the bodies of the hundreds of prisoners who died. The fact that crematoria were built from the start shows that prisoners were expected to die in large numbers in the camps.

Concentration Camps

As soon as the **Nazis** came to power in 1933, they began setting up concentration camps. The camps were used to imprison all kinds of people that the Nazis labeled **undesirable,** from **political** opponents to **Jehovah's Witnesses.** The Nazis said these prisoners were in **protective custody** because they were a threat to Germany. They said prisoners would be re-educated to accept Nazi beliefs and then released. Sometimes this happened. However, more prisoners died in the camps than were released. There were 30,000 deaths recorded in Dachau camp between 1933 and 1945. Many thousands more deaths were unrecorded. This was a camp supposedly built to re-educate people, not kill them.

New Types of Prisoners

By 1935, the Nazis had crushed most political opposition, so fewer politicals were sent to concentration camps. The Nazis discussed shutting down the camps, but instead decided to send different people there. They used the camps to imprison **asocials** and people from **races** they thought of as inferior. The Nazis had very strong, incorrect, ideas about race. They "invented" a pure **Aryan** race for themselves—white, blonde-haired, blue-eyed, and healthy, such as the "ideal" family shown in this poster. The Nazis invented other races, such as Slavs (Poles and people from the Soviet Union), that they saw as sub-human and inferior, and **Jews** that they saw as dangerous. The number of prisoners kept rising, despite the terrible death rates.

Labor Camps

Labor camps, such as the Plaszow camp pictured here, were built near factories or workplaces, such as stone quarries, so the prisoners could be used as cheap labor. However, even here, work was not the most important aim. From the start, the Nazis spoke of *Vernichtung durch Arbeit*— "destruction through work"— when talking about labor camps. People did work, but their living and working conditions were awful, so they did not work well. A doctor who visited the labor camps in Poland in 1940 reported to the **SS:**

> *The rooms are totally unsuitable. They are dark and dirty and full of fleas and lice. There are 75 people in a room 5 meters by 6 meters*

[16 1/2 feet by 19 1/2 feet]: *sleeping on the floor, without straw, lying on top of each other. The roofs leak, the windows have no glass. Three out of every ten workers have no shoes, trousers, or shirts. There is no soap or water and the sick are crammed in with the healthy.*

Death Camps

Death camps were set up in 1941 to kill as many Jewish people as possible, as efficiently as possible. Millions of Jews were already being killed in concentration camps and labor camps. They died from starvation, disease, and exhaustion. They were also worked to death, beaten to death, and executed for various "crimes." However, death camps were different. They had specially designed **gas chambers** for mass killing. There were four main death camps: Chelmno, Belzec, Sobibor, and Treblinka. Death camps could unload and kill each **transport** of Jews within two hours. The camps had few barracks or other buildings—they were not needed. Most

people sent to death camps were killed right away. They did not work, eat, or sleep there. Only a few hundred "work Jews" were left alive to clean out the ovens, bury the ashes of the dead, and sort out and send off their possessions. The official Polish estimates are that at least 2 million Jews and about 52,000 gypsies were killed in just these four camps between December 1941 and October 1943. That total comes to over 20,000 people killed each day, seven days a week. Death camps were also added to the existing camps of Auschwitz and Majdanek. These camps still provided workers, so they had barracks, showers, and other buildings.

Expansion of Germany

This map shows the land taken over by Germany between 1933 and 1941.

Map legend:
- borders in 1933
- extent of German occupation
- Germany in 1933
- Germany by end of 1938
- Germany by end of 1939
- Germany by end of 1940
- Germany by end of 1941
- Countries controlled by or allied to Germany by end of 1941

Marching Across Europe

Hitler and the **Nazis** used the German army to take over more and more land in Europe. The Nazis wanted to set up a new German Europe, a Greater Germany or **Third Reich.** Britain and France declared war on Germany on September 3, 1939, after the Nazis invaded Poland, hoping to stop the expansion. World War II had begun.

More Camps

As the war went on, the camp system grew rapidly and became more complicated. Different types of camps were created to cope with new kinds of prisoners and the demands that war made on people and factories. Some camps contained several types of camps within the main camp.

- Prisoner-of-war camps: As soon as Germany was at war, its army began to take prisoners from the armies it was fighting. The soldiers were supposed to be put in prisoner-of-war camps and treated according to the Geneva Convention—a set of rules written to make sure that enemy soldiers are treated fairly. French and British soldiers were often treated well, although some were used as workers. When the United States joined the war, their soldiers were treated fairly, too. Russian prisoners of war, however, were more likely to be sent to **concentration camps,** starved, or killed because Nazi ideas about **race** classified them as Slavs.

- Transit camps: As the war progressed, Germany steadily took control of more and more of Europe. **Jews** and other non-**Aryans** in **occupied** lands were sent to the camps. The Nazis set up transit camps in occupied countries like France, Holland, and Belgium. Millions of people, mostly Jewish, were held for a short time in transit camps until they could be taken to camps in Poland, which had been made a part of Greater Germany.

- Sub-camps: As concentration camps and **labor camps** grew, smaller camps, often some distance away from the main camp, were set up. These sub-camps were often near a particular factory or farmland so the prisoners could be used as labor. Sub-camps had high death rates, too, so they brought in replacement prisoners from the main camps.

Changing Camps to Help the War

By 1941, the German government had made so many men join the army that it was desperate for workers in factories, especially in those making war goods. Thus, camp prisoners did more and more of the war work.

The Inspector of Concentration Camps from 1940, Richard Glücks, wrote in 1942: "All the camps are asking for prisoners, since they do not have enough to meet the demands for labor. All camp commanders must make sure everyone who can work is doing so."

Conditions in some camps changed to get the most out of their workers. Oswald Pohl, responsible for organizing the work, wrote to all concentration camp **commandants** on May 15, 1943:

The extent and urgency of the work carried out by prisoners needs every prisoner working to the highest standard. Present results must be improved. Prisoners who work hard and behave well will be granted privileges, including more freedom of movement; extra food; money; tobacco; permission to grow their hair.

Auschwitz

Auschwitz was the most complicated of all of the camps. It had a concentration camp (Auschwitz I), a labor camp (Buna/Monowice), and a death camp (Auschwitz-Birkenau). It also had about 40 sub-camps attached to the labor camp. Finally, it had prisoner-of-war camps, close to the factories. This photo, taken by the British from the air in June 1944, shows Auschwitz-Birkenau (top) and Auschwitz I (bottom).

AUSCHWITZ-BIRKENAU COMPLEX
OSWIECIM, POLAND
26 JUNE 1944

Prisoners

There were many different kinds of prisoners in the camps. Both the prisoners and the guards in all of the camps made clear distinctions between different types of prisoners. The camps quickly developed a set "power structure."

Positions of Power

German criminals were most likely to be made **prisoner functionaries.** They were put in charge of other prisoners as *kapos*—in charge of work, or *blockältesters*—in charge of the barracks. The **SS** chose criminals with a violent past, who were most likely to enjoy, or at least not object to, the violence they were expected to hand out to the other prisoners. Rudolph Hoess, the first **commandant** of Auschwitz, said of German criminals: "Almost without exception they had 'high' positions and so were given all the physical necessities of life."

In the Middle

Politicals were in the middle of the prisoner hierarchy. They were above **asocials**—anyone who did not fit in, from homosexuals to alcoholics. People in these two groups might be given "soft," or easy, jobs like working in the camp kitchens. Prisoners who did indoor work were likely to live longer than those who worked outdoors or in the factories. German or German-speaking politicals sometimes worked in the offices or listed the prisoners arriving at camp. The **Nazis** did not value intellectuals—anyone with more than a basic education—very highly, as these people may disagree with Nazi ideals. Even so, the Nazis saw that intellectuals were useful for office work, as record keeping was a vital part of keeping the camp system running.

Classifying Prisoners

Upon arriving at a camp, each prisoner was given a number and a colored triangle to sew onto his or her uniform. Triangles were handed out according to the Nazi classification of prisoners shown on the official Nazi chart at right. Professional criminals had green triangles. Political prisoners and Christian priests had red. Asocials wore black triangles, and gypsies wore brown. **Jehovah's Witnesses** wore purple triangles, and homosexuals wore pink. **Jews** were put into one of the above groups and then given an extra yellow triangle to show they were Jews.

The Sick

Sick people were always treated badly, no matter what their camp classification. If they could not work, they were of no use. Anyone who became ill tried to hide the sickness for as long as possible. Sick prisoners were sent to the hospital were they got little or no medical attention or food. They were left alone to die or get better. Sometimes they were used for medical experiments. The person in this photo was used for experiments that studied survival at high altitudes. He is still wearing the harness used in the experiment.

The Lowest of the Low

The Nazis saw Poles, Russians, gypsies, and Jews—in that order—as separate, inferior **races.** Thus, they had to do the worst jobs and had the worst living conditions and food. The yellow triangle worn by Jewish people marked them for particularly bad treatment. The SS who ran the camps made it clear to the prisoners in charge that they could treat Jews more brutally than anyone else. Many *kapos* were Germans who believed Nazi **propaganda** about inferior races and were happy to mistreat Jews.

Special Cases

Any prisoner who annoyed one of the SS could be killed, even a *kapo*. If a prisoner appeared for **roll call** "improperly dressed," he or she could be punished or shot.

Most camps had Penal Companies—punishment units where prisoners were kept in specially guarded barracks. Very few people survived the punishment units. Prisoners were sent there for so-called crimes, such as smoking a cigarette at work or wearing more clothes than they had been given.

How Camps Were Used

The camps were used in several different ways. They are mostly known for their part in the **Holocaust,** but the **Nazis** used the first camps to imprison **political** opponents and other people they saw as opponents. The early camps were also used to imprison **asocials**—anyone the Nazis said were not supporting the Nazi state. The difference between the camps and ordinary prisons was that people were sent to the camps without trial and without a date for release. The Nazis used several reasons to justify setting up these camps.

Public Safety

The Nazis said they set up **concentration camps** "to keep Germany safe." Why? On February 28, 1933, the *Reichstag,* the German parliament, was set on fire. The Nazis produced a young **Communist** who confessed to starting the fire. The next day, Hitler persuaded the German president to issue an emergency decree, "For the Protection of the People and State." This decree let the **Gestapo** take people into **protective custody** if they might be a danger to Germany. Prisoners had neither the right to a trial, nor a date for release. The Nazis used the law to arrest political opponents, or anyone they felt like arresting, and send them to concentration camps.

Hard Work

The Nazis said that the concentration camps were set up to re-educate their opponents and asocials. Drunks, tramps, beggars, and the unemployed are typical examples of people the Nazis called asocial. Nazi **propaganda** said that if all of these people went to the camps, through hard work and prison routine, they would come to see that Nazi ideas were right. Hard physical work was seen as good for everyone at the time. As soon as they came to power in 1933, the Nazis set up labor service camps where all young men and women at college had to do "labor service." The Nazis said that working hard was a duty that **citizens** owed to Germany. People who did not work were letting the country down.

Release Certificate

In the early days of the camps, some prisoners were released. This photo shows Fritz Echer's release certificate from Dachau camp on January 29, 1934. Released prisoners were closely watched at first. They had to register with the police in the place they went to live and report to the police station weekly, or even daily. If they seemed to be "behaving" themselves, they had to report less and less often.

Re-education

The Nazis said that concentration camp prisoners also needed to be rescued from the wrong ideas they might have been infected with. Werner Schaefer, the **commandant** of Oranienburg concentration camp, said:

> One should not underestimate the difficulty and value of such educational work. The character of many German people has been damaged by fourteen years of poverty, unemployment, and lack of clear leadership.

He wrote a book about re-education in the camps in 1934 in which he said many of the prisoners had thanked him, with tears in their eyes, as they left; several had offered to pay for similar re-education for their sons.

A Genuine Danger?

At first, the Gestapo arrested genuine political opponents. As time passed, the Gestapo arrested people for less and less reason. Bernt Engelmann, a young man in Hitler's Germany, later a journalist, remembers:

> When I was arrested and sent to Anrath prison, I saw the other prisoners only during our daily "walk," fifteen minutes of shuffling round in a circle in a courtyard. We were forbidden to speak, but of course we whispered to each other.

> The man in the cell next to mine, Marinus, a welder from Rotterdam, had been walking his dog one evening. A German patrol came by and the dog barked at them. They shot the dog and took Marinus with them there and then. His family had no idea what had happened to him.

In 1938, an officer from the part of the **SS** that collected information and spied on people, reported with satisfaction that he had many useful informers:

> In a café, a 64-year-old woman said to the person she was sitting with: "Mussolini has more political sense in one of his boots than Hitler has in his brain." Other customers overheard the remark and one made a phone call. Five minutes later she was arrested by the Gestapo.

The Value of Work

The **Nazis** argued that the work done in the camps was valuable. There were various kinds of work that were useful to the **Third Reich,** Hitler's new German empire. It was the prisoners who built the camps and kept them running. They kept the camp buildings and roads repaired and extended the camps so more prisoners could be accommodated. They did the cooking and cleaning and made the clothes and furniture. This kept the running costs of the camps as low as possible, so they were not a burden on the state. The camps also kept the prisoners away from ordinary people.

Cheap Workers

Prisoners worked for the Nazis directly in stone quarries, in workshops in the camps, and in state factories. The **SS** ran several profitable businesses using camp labor. Camp prisoners also farmed nearby land, but most of the food they grew went to the nearest towns, not to the camp kitchens. The profits went to the SS.

Winter Aid

Prisoners in some camps made a variety of small books and toys for children. They were sold in the streets for the *Winterhilfswerk* (Winter Aid), a charity that helped "deserving" poor Germans. Everybody was expected to take their turn doing the selling, as Paul Kremer, a doctor at Auschwitz, noted in his diary: "March 2, 1944: Today the local Party group told me I had to collect again. I had to sell 100 tiny china badges of characters from fairy stories."

Building Works

Albert Speer was an architect who designed buildings for Hitler. Speer designed the Olympic Stadium in Berlin, right. He planned new towns in Germany and estimated he would need 2 billion bricks just for his building work in Berlin in 1938. The German brickyards could only make 350 million bricks. To avoid buying bricks from abroad, Himmler created new camps, such as Buchenwald and Sachsenhausen, to make the bricks that were needed. These camps were built near rock quarries or clay pits for this purpose.

Cheap Labor

Some camp prisoners worked for local businesses that paid the SS. The fee varied over the years but was always low. In 1944, the SS worked out that it cost 1.34 **Reichmarks (RM)** to keep each male prisoner and 1.22 RM for each female per day. They were charging businesses 4 to 6 marks a day for their workers. Auschwitz made between 15 and 20 billion RM from hiring out prisoners in 1944.

War Work

Starting in 1939, when Germany was at war, the Nazis needed workers to replace those who were called into the army and those making war goods.

In April 1942, Oswald Pohl, who was in charge of organizing war work for the camps, wrote: "War means the camp structure and work of the prisoners need to be changed. Work is more important than re-education. This will affect the way the camps are run." On the same day, he told each camp **commandant**:

*Camp commandants are responsible for maximum productivity. They must set work hours, which must be exhausting—full production must be met. There are no limits to the hours of work. Things that shorten working time (meals, **roll calls,** etc.) are to be kept to a minimum. Long marches to and from the camps for meals are banned.*

Pohl also set up a system of rewards for hard-working prisoners. The improved conditions did not apply to **Jewish** people.

Medical Experiments

The **Nazis** used camp prisoners for medical experiments. They saw this as another way the camps could be useful. Experiments did not go on in every camp—it depended on the size of the camp and the interests of the camp doctors. Medical experiments were carried out for three official reasons: to help the army, to help Germany after the war, and to prove the **racial** ideas invented by the Nazis. Camps also tested new drugs for various German companies.

In one set of experiments, prisoners were given **frostbite** by exposing them, naked, to freezing conditions. The frostbite was allowed to develop into gangrene, a deadly infection if untreated. Doctors experimented to find the best treatments for frostbite and gangrene, both of which affected many German soldiers fighting the **Allies.**

SS doctors also used camp patients to teach nurses how to perform operations. After practicing on patients, whose deaths did not matter to the Nazis, they could operate and save the lives of German soldiers.

Experiments were also carried out on common camp diseases, such as **typhus** and various fevers. In Mauthausen, Dr. Karl Gross injected patients with typhus and **cholera** germs to test various new vaccines. Paul Kremer, a doctor at Auschwitz, arrived in the camp on August 30, 1943: "Arrived to find camp in **quarantine**—malaria, typhus, and dysentery are raging." There was still typhus a month later. Kremer also collected lice, which spread the diseases, from the patients for vaccine experiments.

Not an Experiment

While some patients were forced into conditions where they got frostbite as a medical experiment, many more got it as a result of the terrible living and working conditions. This photo shows patients with frostbite, being treated by Red Cross doctors after Auschwitz camp was **liberated.** Many patients in all of the camps were terrified of doctors and hospitals after their years in the camps, and did not want the Red Cross doctors to treat them.

A Healthy Race

Hitler saw children as the future. He believed they would love and obey him in a country full of fit, racially pure Aryans. This view of the future meant there was no room in Germany for the sick, the disabled, or those believed by the Nazis to be racially inferior. Many medical experiments in the camps aimed at finding ways to get rid of so-called racially inferior people. Hitler loved to have his photo taken with beautiful, healthy children. Here he is posing with members of the Hitler Youth.

A Better Germany?

Another set of experiments was intended to work out a way to stop "unfit" people from having children—to sterilize them. To the Nazis, unfit people included non-**Aryans** and the physically and mentally disabled. The Nazis wanted to find a quicker, cheaper way to sterilize people than by operating on each person. They used X rays and chemical injections. Only a few of these prisoners survived.

A different program fed about 100,000 prisoners in Mauthausen, Sachsenhausen, Buchenwald, and Dachau camps a new meatless sausage, which, if safe, would be a cheap food for Germans after the war. All versions of the sausage caused bad stomach upsets and damage to the digestive system, some of it permanent. The idea was abandoned.

Racial Ideas

Some SS doctors collected skeletons and various body parts, such as the brain, to prove Nazi ideas about race. They wanted to prove that the Aryan race, which they had invented for themselves, was truly a race. They also wanted to show that Aryans had stronger skeletons and organs, bigger brains, and were generally better than people of other races. People of certain races as defined by the Nazis were chosen from those in the camps and measured and tested. They were then killed. The bodies that supported Nazi ideas about race were sent to Hitler. He had a collection of skeletons that he planned to use after the war to teach Nazi racial ideas.

Judenfrei

The **Nazis** had a final use for the camps. They did not openly explain this use, although the **SS** and the camp prisoners were well aware of it. The camps were to help make the lands controlled by Germany *Judenfrei*—"Jew Free." In the early 1930s, some prisoners, including **Jews,** were released from the camps. At that time, Jews were being encouraged to emigrate. The Nazis felt that some experience of being in the camps would convince Jews to leave Germany. Those who did not emigrate were rounded up at regular intervals and shut in the camps or in specially created **ghettos.**

Murder in the Camps

In the camps, Jewish people had the worst living and working conditions. Hundreds of them died in the camps every day, from overwork, starvation, and disease. Even more died from brutal beatings or harsh punishments given out by the SS guards. Others were executed—hanged or shot—for crimes such as holding secret meetings or refusing to obey an order. They were also labeled mentally ill and sent to clinics, where they were killed. Franz Ziereis, **commandant** of Mauthausen, said: "About 20,000 prisoners, including real mentally handicapped ones, were sent to Hartseim Institute and gassed." Of course, other prisoners also died in the camps, but the death rates of Jews, Poles, and Slavs were the highest.

Papers and Passes

Every time the German army took more land, it took over more Jewish people as part of the new population. Each time, the Nazis set up anti-Jewish measures. The people of each newly **occupied** country found they needed a lot of passes and documents just to go about their daily lives. They also needed papers proving that they were not Jewish to keep them from being sent to the camps. The certificate shown here states that the Ungerer family in Alsace, France, are pure **Aryans** and not Jewish.

Death Camps

In 1941, Hans Frank, governor of Nazi-occupied Poland, said: "We must exterminate the Jews wherever and whenever we find them, in order to maintain **Reich** control here." Then in January 1942, the Nazis had a meeting in Wannsee, near Berlin, to discuss what they saw as the "Jewish Problem." It was the first time mass murder was openly discussed as the "Final Solution."

At the meeting, Nazi leaders agreed that emigration had failed—they would not succeed in removing Jews through "legal" means. They decided that Jews must be sent east and kept in **labor camps.** In these camps "a large number will drop out through natural wastage." Those who survive "will have to be dealt with accordingly." What the Nazis meant by this was that the Jews would be killed, as efficiently as possible.

A new type of camp, the **death camp,** was set up at Belzec, Chelmno, Sobibor, and Treblinka. In addition, Auschwitz and Majdanek each had a death camp added.

Kurt Gerstein, an SS officer, watched one gassing at Belzec:

The train arrives, 45 wagons with about 6,700 people, about 1,450 of them dead on arrival. They leave their baggage, undress, have their heads shaved, then go into the death chambers. An officer tells them: "Nothing is going to happen to you. Breath in deeply, the gas is needed to strengthen you, because of all the sickness and epidemics." They pack them in 700–800 to a chamber. The engine finally starts and after 32 minutes they are all dead.

Running the Camps

The camps were run by the **SS.** The leader of the SS, Heinrich Himmler, also ran the **Gestapo,** the secret police. Himmler was a friend of Hitler's and one of the first members of the **Nazi** Party. He divided up the SS and made different people responsible for each part, but they did not always work well together.

Himmler's Inspector of **Concentration Camps** from 1934 to 1940 was Theodore Eicke, who made it clear to the guards that they should have no pity for any enemy of the state—that is, any concentration camp prisoner. He told all camp commanders: "It is the duty of every SS man to identify himself, body and soul, with the cause. Every order must be carried out, even the most difficult of them, without hesitation." The camps eventually needed a huge number of SS to run them—6,000 at Auschwitz alone.

Day-to-Day Control

The SS who worked as guards controlled the daily routine of the camps, organized the prisoners, or worked in the offices. Any SS man could punish a prisoner, but the clerks who organized the prisoners' food, transportation, and work could cut themselves off from what went on. The SS men in charge of the prisoners had the most opportunities to treat them badly, and the least chance of pretending they did not know what was going on. They held **roll calls** that lasted several hours, despite blazing heat, pouring rain, or freezing snow. They inspected barracks and prisoners, handing out punishments if everything was not perfect. Prisoners were beaten and humiliated. They could be shot for anything or nothing.

Gas Vans in Chelmno

Not all of the bad jobs were given to prisoners. For example, low-ranking SS men drove the gas vans at Chelmno. One of them, Walter Burmeister, said at his trial after the war:

> When the lorries [vans] were full, the double doors at the back were closed and the exhaust fitted to the inside of the van. I started the engine and let it run until the people inside had suffocated. Then I drove to the burial place. When I got back the van was cleaned out for the next run. I can no longer say what I thought at the time.

One SS guard, questioned after the war, said that it was possible to ask not to take part in the brutality:

> You had to make it sound like a request, due to your weakness, not refusing an order (which would get you shot). If you did this you usually ended up at a desk, where you could ignore what was going on. Of course, it didn't help your career—you didn't get promotion that way.

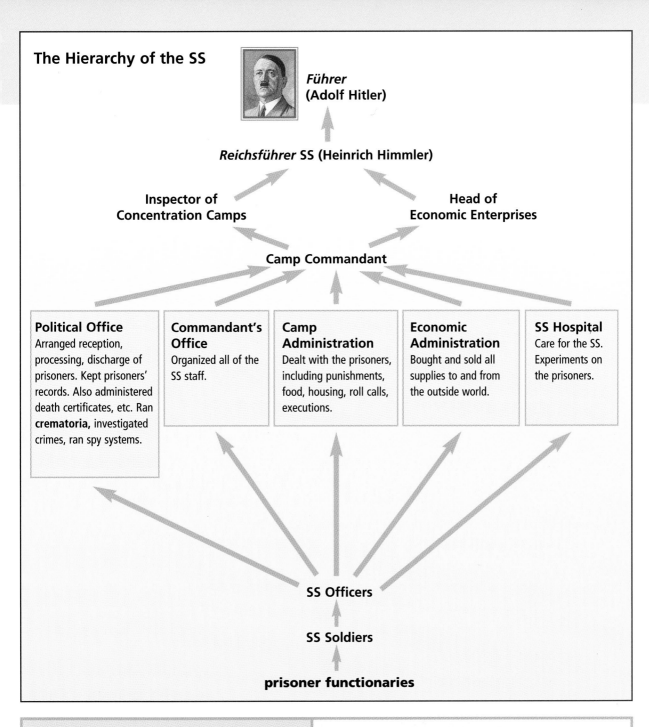

The Hierarchy of the SS

Führer
(Adolf Hitler)

Reichsführer SS (Heinrich Himmler)

Inspector of
Concentration Camps

Head of
Economic Enterprises

Camp Commandant

Political Office
Arranged reception, processing, discharge of prisoners. Kept prisoners' records. Also administered death certificates, etc. Ran **crematoria**, investigated crimes, ran spy systems.

Commandant's Office
Organized all of the SS staff.

Camp Administration
Dealt with the prisoners, including punishments, food, housing, roll calls, executions.

Economic Administration
Bought and sold all supplies to and from the outside world.

SS Hospital
Care for the SS. Experiments on the prisoners.

SS Officers

SS Soldiers

prisoner functionaries

Women

The SS used mainly women officers to run the women's camps. However, women could only go so far in the SS. They were not allowed to be in charge of male camps or even large women's camps. They ran the smaller women's camps and had female ***kapos.*** The SS guards were still men. Johanna Langefeldt became head of the Women's Camp at Auschwitz-Birkenau, under Rudolf Hoess, the **commandant** of all of the Auschwitz camps. Hoess disapproved of Langefeldt and of her *kapos* who he said: "were worse than the men in their toughness, vindictiveness, and depravity. Some were truly repulsive creatures."

Who Was Involved?

Himmler, Eicke, and Pohl were based in offices in Berlin. They were not involved in the brutality of the camps on a daily basis. Even the camp **commandants,** who lived in their camps, could choose not to be involved in the day-to-day brutality of camp life. After the war, Rudolf Hoess, the commandant of Auschwitz, suggested that camp commandants were not really the ones who ran the camps:

> *I wanted to get useful work out of the prisoners, so wanted to give them better treatment than was usual in **concentration camps.** But my efforts to do this were in vain because the officers ran the camp in the Eicke way. The real ruler of every concentration camp is not the camp commander, but the officer in charge of the camp. It was this officer who taught his men how to behave, and it was they who taught the **kapos,** from the chief block leader down to the last block clerk, how to behave.*

This was, clearly, an attempt to excuse his involvement in the **Holocaust.**

Careful Choice of Words

Most **Nazis** used words like "filth" and "vermin" to make **Jews** seem less like people. They also used words to cover up acts of cruelty and mass murder. They used these words in documents to hide what they were doing. They also used them in conversation—as a way of not looking clearly at what was going on. They used the terms "special treatment" and "disinfection" to refer to killing prisoners. They said prisoners were on "work detail," when really they were being given pointless, dangerous jobs to do to work them to death. "Special actions" were mass gassings or mass shootings. "Natural wastage" meant prisoners dying through the terrible camp conditions. However, not everyone was always so careful. Karl Jager, head of ***Einsatzkommando*** 3, an **SS** death squad sent into Russia behind the invading German army to murder Jews, reported in December 1941: "I now want to bump off the 'work Jews' and their families—all that remain in my area."

One of the SS guards at Treblinka **death camp** had a St. Bernard dog called Barry. He taught the dog to attack Jewish prisoners when he gave the order: "Man, bite the dog!" Another guard said at his trial: "By 'man' he meant the dog, Barry, and by 'dog' he meant the prisoners." He did not try to hide his contempt for Jewish people. He went out of his way to make things even more unbearable for them.

Working in the Camps

The head of the Economic and Administrative Office, Oswald Pohl, had to make sure the camps made a profit. In 1938, he set up the first SS-controlled company, the German Earth & Stone Works. More SS companies, like this one painted by a survivor, were set up, all making a good profit. Pohl also hired out workers to German companies. Pohl wanted prisoners who were fit to work and who work well. This plan clashed with Eicke's system of brutal punishments and bad working and living conditions. Yves Beon, a French prisoner in the Dora camp, remembered:

> Since March 13, 1944, the death rate has been high, with no incoming people. The population is dropping, yet the work must increase. The SS believe the perfect cure for the drop in numbers is—more beatings! With a good club, miracles can be worked, as long as an expert is using it.

Room to Move

Kapos and other prisoner functionaries had better living conditions. This is a **blockältester's** room in Auschwitz I **concentration camp.** *Blockältesters* were in charge of the other prisoners in the barracks. This amount of space was a huge luxury—ordinary prisoners were stacked three or more to a bunk.

Prisoner Functionaries

The **SS** used prisoners to do the day-to-day organizing of other prisoners. These **prisoner functionaries** lived longer. Some filled in forms or organized the kitchen stores, but most prisoner functionaries had to make other prisoners do something, often by beating them. The SS gave these jobs to "green" prisoners, that is, prisoners who wore a green triangle on their uniforms to show they were in prison for committing a crime, not for **political** or **racial** reasons. Green prisoners were mainly German criminals who did not mind the violence, and who even shared the **Nazis'** hatred of **Jews,** Poles, and Slavs, and were happy to beat them up. They were still prisoners, though, and life for them was not safe. The SS gave them power, but could take it away at any time. As a prisoner from

Dora said: "They had armbands and warm clothes and boots, but they knew they would die, too, one way or another. Even after eight years they still had fear eating away at them."

Kapos were prisoners who were put in charge of other prisoners. In most camps, the *kapos* were organized by a *Lagerältester*—a camp leader. A prisoner from Mauthausen later explained the system:

> The SS Kommandoführer [leader of a work squad] *told the SS men under him what work their part of the squad had to do each day. The SS then told the* kapos *what they wanted done. Each* kapo, *or one of his* hilfskapo [assistant kapo], *"encouraged" a prisoner to do his job with bull whips, rubber clubs, rods, and so on.*

Blockältesters

Each barracks had a *blockältester* who had to get everyone up on time and ready for **roll call.** They made sure the prisoners kept themselves and their barracks as clean as possible and gave out the food. In return, depending on the size of the camp, each *blockältester* had his own room, or at least his own bed. Hugo Gryn, sent to Auschwitz as a teenager, remembers his first meeting with a *blockältester*:

> *He was a fairly young man with an armband marked "Blockälteste 7." He had two assistants and the three of them lined us up in "proper order," as they called it. There were about 700 of us and by the time we had "learned" how to line up, dismiss, and line up again, we were exhausted and very hungry.*

The *blockältester* and his assistants went and fetched the food. The prisoners were each given a small piece of bread with a spoonful of jam on it and told that it had to last 24 hours.

Prisoners also worked in the administration buildings, filling in forms and typing orders or reports. Sometimes they had more difficult work. Tadeusz Sobolewicz, a Polish prisoner who spoke German, had to register Jews who were not sent straight to their deaths in the **gas chambers** at Auschwitz-Birkenau.

> *I had to write almost without pause. "Where and when were you born? Name? Where do you want your letters sent?" It was hard work and I knew it wasn't needed, any of this information. From time to time I would look one of them in the eye— did they know? That night I couldn't sleep. I could see the red glow in the sky where they were burning the relatives of the people I had processed.*

This photo, taken by the SS, shows prisoners like Tadeusz Sobolewicz waiting to process new arrivals to Auschwitz.

25

The Worst Work

Death camps, like Auschwitz-Birkenau, used *kapos* in **selection**—deciding who would live and who would die as people climbed off the trains. On August 11, 1942, about 1,000 men, women, and children arrived in Auschwitz-Birkenau from Sosnowitz **Ghetto.** Only 46 men were chosen to live. **SS** men did the choosing, but the *kapos* got people into line, forced families apart, unloaded the baggage, and took it to be sorted. As part of the unloading process, they had to drag out dead bodies and search the filthy wagons for valuables. Then they had to clean both the wagons and the platform.

A Helping Hand

Some *kapos* were able to help prisoners. They knew what was going to happen to new arrivals. In Auschwitz-Birkenau some new arrivals were sent straight to their deaths, while others were kept alive for a while as workers. *Kapos* knew how those who were selected for work were chosen, so they could sometimes help someone survive. Doing so was a big risk—if they were caught they would have been shot or sent to the **gas chambers.** Hugo Gryn remembers how a *kapo* saved his life:

> *The men in striped trousers took away the luggage. I didn't want to give up my rucksack* [backpack]. *The man who took it away from me said something in Polish. I replied in German that I did not understand. "You are nineteen and you are a mechanic, or something like it! Don't forget, nineteen!" As he said this to me, he kept looking sideways in case he was seen talking.*

Hugo told his father, who said he should do as the man said. Hugo was selected for work.

Selection

This photo of selection in Auschwitz-Birkenau, taken by the SS, shows the early stages in the selection process for a **transport** of Jews from Hungary in 1944. You can see an SS officer (in the peaked cap), an SS guard (behind the officer), and the *kapos* (in the striped uniforms) waiting to empty the train.

Sonderkommando

The *Sonderkommando*, or Special Detachment, were **Jewish** men who were forced to take people to the gas chambers, remove the corpses from the gas chambers, and burn them in the **crematoria** ovens. Anyone refusing to do this work was sent straight to the gas chambers with the next transport. The *Sonderkommando* did not take part in the gassing itself. Rudolf Hoess, **commandant** at Auschwitz, explained that it was important to have *Sonderkommando* prisoners there:

> *The calm behavior of the Special Detachment reassured those who were worried or suspicious about what was going on. They might not believe the SS, but they would believe one of their own* **race.**

Hoess said that the *Sonderkommando* cooperated in creating calm: "They lied to the new arrivals very convincingly. I never heard of any of them telling, or even hinting, of what lay ahead."

Keeping a Record

Some members of the *Sonderkommando* wrote down what was going on in the death camps. They hid their records in different places, hoping that they would be found. This picture shows some pages of a description of the way the gas chambers of Auschwitz-Birkenau worked. They were hidden in the metal flask at the top of the picture.

Doomed Themselves

The *Sonderkommando* were kept alive for varying amounts of time in different camps—the average was about four months. During this time, some died from starvation, brutality, and disease, although they had better living conditions because of the work they did. The SS regularly killed them to make a revolt less likely, leaving only enough alive to teach the newcomers their jobs.

Camp Discipline

The **Nazis** believed in hard work, discipline, and obedience. They expected ordinary Germans to follow these rules. Prisoners in **concentration camps** had to be even more hard working and even more obedient. There were millions of prisoners in the camps and not many **SS** to control them. So how did the SS control prisoners?

Camp Rules

The SS had all of the advantages—they were fit, well fed, and had guard dogs and weapons. They were still worried about revolts in the camps. The first thing they did was to make it hard for the prisoners to get together in groups. The camp rules gave the death penalty to anyone "discussing politics, having meetings, forming groups, loitering with others, persuading others to commit a crime,

encouraging mutiny." Prisoners had to make meeting each other accidental and keep conversations short. However, the SS knew that it would still be possible, if difficult and dangerous, for prisoners to meet and make plans in secret.

Prisoner Against Prisoner

The SS then made it difficult for prisoners to trust each other. They put prisoners in charge of other prisoners and encouraged different kinds of prisoners to hate each other. The **commandant** of Auschwitz, Rudolph Hoess, said:

*We encouraged various groups to see each other as enemies—we did everything we could to encourage not only the **political** differences, but also other antagonisms between various groups of prisoners. This made it much less likely that they would all join together against us.*

Towers and Fences

Prisoners were physically controlled and watched in the camps. Concentration camps were designed so that every part of the camp could be watched from one of the lookout towers that were built along the fence that kept everyone in. This photograph was taken standing beside one lookout tower, looking toward the next.

Keeping Moving

The SS kept everyone moving around the camps, mainly using cattle wagons like this one. Each time prisoners were moved, they had to be taken off one set of camp lists, go through the whole arrival process again, and be put on the lists in the new camp. The SS had more work—arranging the **transports** and keeping the records straight—but they thought the work was worth it. They had found another way to stop resistance groups from forming. It also unsettled prisoners. All camp routines were similar, but moving prisoners meant they did not settle into a routine with familiar faces.

Of course, it was also dangerous to be an informer. It was easier for prisoners to kill an informer in their barracks or on their work gang than it was for them to kill a **kapo** or an SS guard. Informers had to rely on the SS for protection. They seldom got it, as the SS could always find a new informer.

Eyes Everywhere

Prisoners were encouraged to tell the SS guards of any plots they overheard, in the same way as people outside the camp were encouraged to inform on **Jews** or **undesirables** among their neighbors. In the camps, being an **informer** brought real benefits. Camp informers were given more food or easier jobs, just for watching and listening. They got even better rewards if they uncovered a plot, so it was hard for prisoners to trust each other.

Shifting People

Other things stopped people from forming settled groups. The SS deliberately changed work groups around. There was less need to move people around in the barracks—there were so many people crammed into each barrack that there was not enough privacy to plot against the SS. The camp population changed from other factors, too. People died in the camps all the time, either killed by the SS or from disease, starvation, or overwork.

A System of Punishment

The **concentration camp** rules set out a clear system of punishments. They were first used in Dachau, then applied in all camps. Here are some of them:

Punishments allowed at any time are: beatings, drilling, no mail or food, tying to stakes, reprimands, and warnings.

3 days solitary confinement for anyone who:
- Does not get up at once, or does not keep his bed or room in proper order.
- Takes a second helping of food without permission, or allows the cooks to give him two helpings.

5 days solitary confinement for anyone who:
- Sits or lies on his bed during the day without permission.

8 days solitary confinement (and a whipping of 25 strokes before and after) for anyone who:
- Makes ironical remarks about an **SS** officer, or who does not show respect or in any other way does not do as he is told.
- Given authority by the SS, abuses this by favoring, making false reports on, or tyrannizing other prisoners.

The following will be hanged:
- Anyone who, at any point, discusses politics; forms a **political** group; loiters with others; collects true or false information about the concentration camps or takes such information, buries it, passes it on to others, smuggles it out of the camp, discusses it after release, or gets it outside the camp by throwing it over the wall; tries, by climbing onto barrack roofs or up trees, to contact the outside world with signals, lights, or so on; tries to escape, commit a crime, or persuade anyone else to do so.
- Anyone who attacks a guard or SS man; refuses to obey an order; encourages mutiny; leaves a marching column or place of work; shouts, agitates, or makes speeches on the march or at work.

Bending the Rules

The examples on page 30 suggest that the camp rules were clear, but in reality, anything could be turned into a punishment, and punishment could be handed out for any reason. The rules varied from SS guard to SS guard. For example, prisoners were supposed to report for **roll call** "properly dressed." Some SS might punish those appearing without a cap with a beating. Others would shoot the "improperly dressed" prisoner. A standard punishment was 25 lashes of a whip or stick. However, many SS men made the prisoners count the 25 lashes themselves, in German. If the prisoner lost count they had to go back to the beginning. Many prisoners could not speak any German before they arrived in the camps.

Punished for the "Crimes" of Others

When a prisoner escaped, the SS punished the remaining prisoners. In Auschwitz I in 1940, a prisoner was missing at noon roll call. A punishment roll call was ordered. The prisoners stood, at attention, from noon until 9 P.M. without coats, hats, or shoes. The missing prisoner was found dead, having crawled into a doorway to find shelter from the sleet. After the roll call there were 120 prisoners dead, sick, or unconscious.

Once it was certain that a prisoner had escaped, the SS often executed some of the remaining prisoners. They often did this on significant days. For instance, Polish Catholics were executed on important Christian holidays or on Polish national holidays.

A Different Kind of Hanging

These prisoners are being punished by being hanged from posts. To the SS this was a mild punishment, so their crimes had probably been small—like not working fast enough. Although the SS saw the punishment as mild, it was torture. Prisoners hanged for several hours, at least. They lost all feeling in their hands, feet, and legs. They were often beaten by guards or attacked by guard dogs while they hung, as in this picture. This picture was painted in 1946 by Wladyslaw Siwek, an ex-prisoner who, after the war, worked as an artist for the Auschwitz-Birkenau State Museum.

Prisons

Camps were prisons in themselves, but many of the camps had prisons or punishment units attached to them. These "Penal Companies" formed part of the camp discipline system. They were run by the **"Political"** section of the camp **SS.**

Prisoners were sent to the prison block for imprisonment in solitary confinement. People from outside the camp who tried to help prisoners, or who resisted the **Nazis** in other ways, were also sometimes brought to camp prisons for execution.

People who tried to escape, or escaped and were recaptured, were locked up in the prison until they could be publicly executed. The ordinary cells were bad enough. Bare rooms of about 20 feet by 7 feet (3 meters by 2 meters) had between ten and twenty prisoners crowded into them with just one small high window for ventilation. Auschwitz I also had standing cells, just 3 feet by 3 feet (1 meter by 1 meter). As many as four prisoners were crammed into one of these cells, where it was impossible to do anything but stand. Pery Broad, an SS officer, described the standing cells after the war:

> *Many prisoners spent terrible hours, even weeks, standing there in the dark. They could not sit down, or move about when it was cold. Breathing was almost impossible. A sentence here was almost certain death.*

Executions

This execution wall between Block 10 (the medical experiment block) and Block 11 (the prison) in Auschwitz I is where prisoners were shot. Prisoners were also hanged. One guard remembered the process: "It went like this: one—to the stool; two—on the stool; three—read the sentence; they had to put their own head in the noose; four—stool pulled out. I pulled out one stool."

No Escape?

The SS always made a show of recapturing people who had escaped. Sometimes they took prisoners from the nearest town jail and pretended that they were the escapees, so prisoners would think that no one ever got away. When they did this, the SS made sure that they executed the "escapees" quickly, so no one had a chance to get a close look at them. Recaptured prisoners were marched back into camp, with everyone lined up to watch. They had to sing happy songs as they entered the camp or, as in this picture drawn by a prisoner, wear a board saying "Here we are again!" or "Hurrah, we're back."

Punishment Units

The camp rules said: "Punitive [punishment] work will be severe physical or particularly dirty work, performed under close supervision." Prisoners in these units were not only given the hardest kind of work, they were expected to do this work while running. After their day's work they were given extra work in the evening—again, heavy manual work. Punishment units had from 150 to 600 prisoners in them at any time. While the prisoners worked harder, they were given less food than ordinary prisoners. It is not surprising that many died. Most work companies carried home several dead each day. Day after day, the Penal Company would take an empty cart to work and bring it back full of dead bodies.

Women, Too

Both men and women could be put into punishment units. The women's Penal Company of Auschwitz was set up in the village of Budy, about 2.5 miles (4 kilometers) from Auschwitz, in June 1942. There were 200 prisoners at first. Elfriede Runge ran the camp with 25 guards and dogs and about 20 female **kapos.** The women in this camp did mainly heavy manual work: cleaning out ponds, digging drainage ditches, and repairing roads.

Efficient Camps

The **Nazis** wanted the camps to work efficiently and to pay for themselves, or even make a profit. They were not to be a burden on the state—that is, cost the government anything to run. Early **SS** efficiency measures were relatively logical. As the war went on, they became less and less so.

Bureaucracy

In the Nazi system, everything had to be accounted for and everything needed the right kind of **authorization.** The **commandant** of the Auschwitz camps, Rudolf Hoess, found this affected his camps:

In Berlin they were arguing over who would pay to build the camp. I had permission to build and prisons begging to send me prisoners, yet I could not get even 100 yards [91 meters] of barbed wire. There were mountains of barbed wire in the nearest Engineering Depot.

But I could not touch it without authorization from Berlin. So I had to steal it, dismantling old fortifications and using all the steel, wire, and other materials that I could.

Cheap Workers

The SS used the prisoners in the camp as cheap labor. They hired them out to local businesses and, later, used them in SS-run factories, quarries, and mines. The prisoners were a cheap labor force because they were not paid wages—the businesses paid the SS, not the prisoners. One of the SS officers in charge of the use of camp inmates, Karl Somer, said: "There were about 500,000 camp prisoners working in German industry as a whole in 1941." Prisoners were also cheap because the SS spent the absolute minimum on feeding, housing, and clothing them. The SS Hygienic Institute even worked out recipes for the most economical bread and soup.

Cheap to Keep

Early prisoners in **concentration camps** slept on straw on the floors. Later, camp commandants introduced bunks, but not to improve conditions for the prisoners or to give them a better night's sleep. It was because with an average of three to each bunk, they could fit more prisoners into the same space.

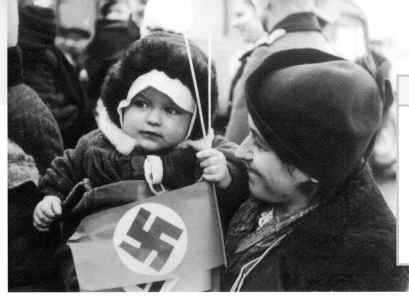

Resettlement

Jewish homes and business were handed over to non-Jewish people. This photo shows a German mother and child arriving in Poland to be resettled.

Stolen Possessions

The Nazis sold all of the possessions left behind by **Jews** who emigrated, went into hiding, or were taken to camps and **ghettos.** Sometimes, the possessions were given to Germans as part of the Nazi Welfare program. They called these possessions "left-over Jewish effects" or "goods taken from Jewish thieves."

The Eigis family were Germans **resettled** in Poland when Germany took over Estonia. The Nazi theory was that once they took over a country, German people should be moved in to begin to make the new land part of Germany. This policy, implemented by the SS, was called "Germanization." The Eigis family were moved to Poland and lived for a while in a transit camp in an old school. Then one day:

> *We were given the keys to a flat*
> [apartment] *and were told how to get there. The people had left quickly, drawers were open, beds still unmade, food on the table. We found a small restaurant run by Poles and told the Nazis about it. They signed it over to us. We felt guilty. But we had to survive. We had to make a living.*

Counting Every Reichmark

The SS in Auschwitz I charged the company I. G. Farben the correct price for transporting prisoners and guards to and from the Farben works each day from the camp. They did not want to cheat Farben, but they did not want the national train system to lose money either. This is how they worked it out:

> *Feb 28, 1942: There is room for 100 workers in each car. To calculate the cost of travel, the number of prisoners and supervisors* [armed SS guards] *transported daily is worked out. Charges are based on the price of a third class monthly ticket for up to 10 kilometers* [6.2 miles] *for each person* [just over 0.28 **Reichmark (RM)** each]. *By the end of December 1941, 158,569 people had made the journey. Cost: 45,636.80 RM.*

The SS would have already made about 600,000 RM from their charges for the workers, depending on how many guards were on the trains and how skilled the workers were. Yet, they still worked out the fare to the exact 0.80 RM.

More Soldiers Needed

As the war dragged on, **Nazi** ideas of efficiency became more extreme. More soldiers were needed and more war workers, too. The number of **SS** guards had to be reduced and the number of workers increased. Also, as the Nazis moved from persecuting Jewish people to the mass murdering of them, the SS were told to find more and more efficient ways of killing people and disposing of the bodies.

In February 1942, Richard Glücks, Inspector of **Concentration Camps,** ordered that fewer prisoners should clean and maintain the camp—even the sick now had to do this, to free workers for the war effort.

More soldiers were needed at the front, so Glücks wanted to find a way to keep prisoners in the camps, while taking out as many of the guards as possible to send to fight. Rudolph Hoess remembered:

He insisted on more and more economies, replacing men with electrified wire, dogs, and minefields. Anyone who could work out a more efficient way of cutting guard numbers was promoted at once. He even imagined that dogs could be trained to circle around the prisoners, as if they were sheep, to prevent them from escaping. One sentry, with the help of several dogs, was supposed to guard 100 prisoners safely.

Selling Tickets

The Nazis insisted that **Jewish** people had to have a one-way **resettlement** ticket for the trains that took them to the **death camps.** The tickets were paid for by the people themselves, the Jewish community they were taken from, or, as a last resort, by the German state. Children were half price. People were even told that group bookings could be arranged. Partly, these tickets were a Nazi trick to reassure the Jews that they were being sent somewhere worth going to. It was also another example of the Nazis trying to make as much money out of the

Jewish people as they could. The tickets shown here, printed in German and Greek, were bought for some of the 55,000 Greek Jews **transported** to Auschwitz-Birkenau.

Hair

These rolls of cloth have been analyzed by scientists who found that they were made from human hair. Richard Glücks insisted that: "The cut human hair in all concentration camps is to be utilized." Men's hair was to be made into felt and yarn. Women's hair was to be made into yarn, socks for submarine crews, and hair-felt stockings for workers on the German railroad. The camp **commandants** had to send in lists, on the fifth of every month, of the "amounts of hair collected monthly, separated into male and female hair." This went on at all camps.

The commander of Mauthausen, Franz Ziereis, describing the camp to U.S. soldiers after his capture at the end of the war, said: "In almost all camps, the hair of the men, women, children was cut so it could be used for felt boots."

War Economies

Possessions were carefully recycled from the moment Jews were first forced to give them up. As the war caused shortages, the recycling became more organized. Scissors were shipped to SS barber shops and razors and razor blades to SS pharmacies for resale.

Medicines and medical equipment went to army hospitals. The local SS quickly used any expensive food that was seized, while ordinary food went to feed the guards.

The "Final Solution"

Once the Nazis decided on the "Final Solution"—killing all Jews—to what they called the "Jewish Problem," they wanted to put it into practice as efficiently as possible. This meant killing more people, more quickly, for less cost and less emotional disturbance for the people who did the killing. They also wanted to make as much profit out of every single corpse as they could. So they had to reuse not only that person's possessions, but also their hair, teeth, and fillings—everything.

Personal Profit

When possessions were taken from **Jewish** people, any German money found was supposed to go straight to the **SS** bank in Berlin. Other money, jewelry, and precious metals were sent to the *Reichsbank,* as profit for the German state. Less valuable possessions were given out as state welfare to needy Germans. Watches, pens, clothes, shoes—everything—was collected, sorted, stored, and transported from place to place. Many surviving documents show that this happened on a huge scale. In 1943, Auschwitz was shipping 20 loaded wagons of goods a day to Germany.

With all of this activity, there were opportunities for stealing on every level. It was seen as stealing from the German state, though, and was punishable by death. Many people took the risk of getting caught. A ***kapo*** might steal a pair of shoes or some food. A guard might steal a watch. The higher in the SS ranks a person was, the more chance there was for making a big personal profit to hide away until after the war.

Profit from Corpses

The SS wanted to make as much money out of the Jews as it could. They worked out the most efficient way to kill as many Jews as possible, as cheaply as possible. Once the Jews were dead, the SS cut off and reused any hair and took out all gold teeth and fillings. Auschwitz had a special laboratory for melting these fillings and making gold bars. They searched the bodies carefully to make sure there were no valuables hidden on them. Lastly, they got rid of them as efficiently as possible. The German company that made the gas ovens that burned the bodies, Topf & Sons, was under pressure to keep redesigning the ovens to take more bodies, burn them faster, and use less fuel.

Babies

The SS saw Jewish babies and young children as economically worthless. Once the Final Solution was adopted, they were sent straight to the **gas chambers.** Before, they might have been killed or left to starve to death. This photo shows some of the baby and toddler clothes that had not been recycled when the Russians **liberated** Auschwitz.

Unmatched Shoes

These are just a few of the shoes found at Auschwitz when it was liberated. They are not paired up, and there are so many of them that it would have been impossible to match them up once they were all bundled into heaps in the barracks.

While the SS sent in reports about how many thousands of pairs of shoes were being "stored for reuse," their system was actually falling apart. There were too many people passing through the camp for their workers to sort the goods.

Really Efficient?

Official records show how possessions were reused, but these records do not tell the whole story. They present the camp officials as more organized than they really were, especially toward the end of the war. The idea of efficiency was there, just as the **Nazi** leaders were still saying Germany would win the war. Reality was very different, though, as people scrambled to save themselves. As more and more Jews arrived at Auschwitz to be gassed, there was no longer enough room in the warehouses for all of their possessions. Bundles were stacked up outside, piled several feet high.

When it was clear that Soviet troops were advancing into Poland, the SS tried to destroy the evidence of the **death camps** and retreat. They had to leave Auschwitz in a hurry.

The Nazis only managed to partially destroy the gas chambers and the area of the camp where they stored all of the belongings they had taken. What survived shows that, toward the end of the war, everything was still saved, but it was not properly sorted or stored. For example, heaps of eyeglasses were found, their frames rusty and their lenses broken.

Processing Arrivals at Auschwitz

All new arrivals in the camps were processed in much the same way. The next few pages tell how things were done at the Auschwitz **concentration camps.**

Transportation

Most prisoners arrived by train, 80 or more crammed into locked cattle wagons. The journey could take hours or days. The prisoner **transports** often had to wait while transports of soldiers and equipment used the main line. There was no air in summer and no heat in winter in the wagons. However long the journey took, the prisoners were not given any food or water. Some were given a bucket to use as a toilet—others did not even get that. People died in almost every wagon, every day. Soldiers guarded the trains to make sure that no one escaped.

Trucks

Some prisoners arrived in trucks. Jerzy Tabeau, a Polish **political** prisoner, described his journey to Auschwitz I from prison:

In the yard are two small trucks. Thirty of us get into each one. The first in stand stooped over (it is too low to stand up) next to the front wall of the truck. This first layer is about 15 people. The next in sit with their legs spread wide in front of them. This is so that one man can sit between the legs of the one behind, so 30 people are fitted into a space 2 meters by 1.5 meters [6 1/2 feet by 4 feet]. They cram us in with rifle butts,

*beating, and shouting. In the free half of the truck stand two **SS** men with submachine guns. There are three armed motorcycle guards, too. The trucks are covered and off we go. The trip lasts one and a half hours and we are all numb at the end of it. We are beaten out of the trucks, with no allowance for the fact we find it hard to move.*

Armed SS men with attack dogs unloaded the transports. The SS deliberately made arrival noisy and confusing. Then they beat prisoners for not understanding and obeying their orders. These orders were in German, not the native language of the arriving prisoners. All through the process the SS beat the prisoners, cursed them, and snapped out orders in German.

Death Camps

Death camps processed arrivals differently from concentration camps and **labor camps.** People were transported to the camps in trains, and no records were made of the arrivals. Death camps only had barracks for the **Nazis** who ran them and the hundred or so *Arbeitsjuden*—"work **Jews**" who sorted the possessions of the dead, cleared out the **gas chambers,** and buried or burned the bodies. Arrivals were stripped and herded straight to the gas chambers. Sometimes there were lists of the names, sometimes not. Prisoners were not given numbers and did not appear on camp records. They were in the camps for an average of two hours before they died.

An Easier Journey

When smaller numbers were transported, conditions could be easier, especially if there were guards in the same van. When Hugo Gryn, who arrived in Auschwitz as a teenager, was taken from Auschwitz to Lieberose, a sub-camp of Sachsenhausen, guards traveled with them: "Fifty prisoners were ordered into each wagon with three fully armed SS men. Twenty-five on one side and twenty-five on the other. The middle space was left for the guards."

The train traveled all night. The guards were the last to wake in the morning. As soon as the train stopped, they opened the doors to let in some air. The prisoners were then ordered out of the wagon: "We were lined up, five by five. The guards took their places on either side, with rifles leveled horizontally, and we set off."

New Arrivals

This painting, made by a prisoner after the war, shows new arrivals being lined up in Auschwitz I camp. The arrivals, all men of a wide range of ages, are still in their own clothes with their possessions in cases and bundles. An officer is shouting orders at the new arrivals, while a prisoner stands at the front to show how to follow these orders properly. The officer has a whip, while the sergeant and the **kapo** at the back of the rows have sticks to beat the prisoners with.

Worthless Lives

Once prisoners were unloaded and their possessions had been taken away, the process of turning them from people into numbers began. Each stage was made as humiliating as possible, to show the prisoners how little their lives were worth. Families who had traveled together were separated into two lines: one of men and one of women with children. Arek Hersh, a young **Jewish** boy sent to Auschwitz from the Lodz **Ghetto,** remembers that after the groups had been split up:

*We men were marched to a small square, surrounded by electric fencing and some barracks. We were told to stop and form rows. We did so and stood there for about an hour, facing a doorway. Suddenly, the door opened and a group of naked women with their heads shaved ran out, herded by **SS** men with whips. They were the wives and daughters of some of the men in our group. It was degrading, sickening, and shaming to watch the SS men beat these women.*

Undressing

First, the prisoners had to take off their clothes. If they were arriving for the first time, they had to put their clothes in a paper bag that they had to hand in for storage until their release—at least, this is what they were told. If they were being moved from one prison to another, they just handed in their old prison uniform. Once they were naked, prisoners were often left for a long time, sometimes hours. Sometimes they had to go through the whole process running. The SS were making the point that things would be done when it suited them, without any thought for the comfort of the prisoners.

Dividing People Up

These new arrivals at Auschwitz camp have been divided into two lines, male and female. Strong young men, especially those who had a useful skill, such as carpentry or metalworking, were the kind of workers the SS wanted most.

Showers

These prisoners were photographed by the SS leaving the shower in Auschwitz-Birkenau. Hugo Gryn remembers that his arrival also included a chemical wash to prevent lice:

The hall had a cement floor. A few inches below the ceiling were pipes with holes in them. When we were all in, the showers were turned on. Within a few seconds everyone was soaking wet. I enjoyed it. I washed Dad's back and he washed mine. Suddenly the water stopped to be replaced a few seconds later with ice cold water. Then we had to go into another hall. As

we went through, a man ran spongy gloves all over our heads and the other places where hair grows. The liquid on the sponges was awful, for two minutes I could not get my breath back, and the places he mopped felt as if they were on fire.

Shaving

Prisoners were then taken to the next room, where they were shaved. The hair on their heads was shaved off, as well as all of the other hair on their bodies. Shaving was supposed to stop lice, which live in human hair, from spreading. It was also a chance to humiliate the prisoners. A French singer, Fania Fénelon, remembers being shaved on arrival at Auschwitz:

A young Polish woman hacked desperately at my two, thick, jet-black plaits [braids] with blunt scissors. She then attacked my head, armpits, and other hair with an old

*rusty blade and no soap and water. She clawed and scraped. It should have hurt badly, but I don't remember—I was watching another **kapo** who had picked up my plaits [braids] and was playing with them, taunting me.*

Shaved prisoners were sent to the showers. Here again the SS played cruel games— they made the showers boiling hot or icy cold, or both, one after the other. Prisoners were not given a towel to dry off with after the showers, but herded on, still wet, to the next stage of the process.

Uniforms

Prisoners were given prison uniforms once they were showered. Most often, they were given a striped camp uniform, like the ones in this photo. However, if these had run out, they were given clothes from a previous transport of prisoners. These clothes had a stripe painted on them. Whatever they were given to wear was usually full of lice, making the disinfection they had just gone through pointless. Whenever possible, the clothes the prisoners were given did not fit, in order to make them look ridiculous. Most were issued wooden clogs to wear on their feet, oversized if possible. Prisoners found it harder to walk and keep in step with these shoes, giving the SS another opportunity to punish them.

Registration

The prisoners also had to be registered. A **kapo** wrote their details—name, address, nationality, relatives, job, and so on—on a form. The forms were kept by the **Political** division of the camp **SS.** They made ten to twenty copies of lists of the prisoners and sent the copies to different offices in the camp and in Berlin.

Tadeusz Sobolewicz, a Polish political prisoner who spoke German, had to register the **Jews** at Auschwitz-Birkenau who did not go straight to the **gas chambers:**

*The SS man handed out thick wads of forms. He spent a long time explaining the information we had to get from the prisoners and where to write it down. We were warned: "You're only allowed to ask questions. Fill in the forms, don't talk, tell them nothing." The first **transport** was from Holland. There was a stream of men coming to our tables. I had to write almost without pause. "Where and when were you born? Name? Where did you live? Where do you want your letters sent?" It was hard work and I knew it wasn't needed, any of this information.*

Just a Number

Once prisoners were registered, they were given a number. In all of the camps, prisoners were given a number to sew onto their clothing. In some camps, they were also given a number to wear around their wrists. From that point on, they were never spoken to by name, just by number.

Sometimes it could be useful not being seen as a person. Tadeusz Sobolewicz was caught sleeping in the daytime by the SS and was told to report to the Penal Company. Most people sent to this punishment unit died within days. Tadeusz's friends managed to swap his uniform with the uniform of a dead prisoner. He lived pretending to be the dead prisoner for a few days. His friends, who knew a clerk in the offices, got the clerk to switch numbers to make it seem that the dead man, not Tadeusz, had been sent to the Penal Company. This would not have been possible if the SS had seen their prisoners as people, not numbers.

Tattoos

In Auschwitz, from 1942 on, prisoners also had their number tattooed onto their arm. Auschwitz was the only camp to tattoo prisoners. There were so many prisoners and the death rate was so high—sometimes several hundred a day—that tattooing was necessary. Tattoos made it easier for the SS to keep track of all of the prisoners.

Prisoner Photographs

Most **death camps** simply made lists of the prisoners. In Auschwitz, they also photographed most of their early prisoners. Some of the photos, like this set, survived and are in Auschwitz I, which is now a state museum. Most Jews were not photographed and, as the war went on, supplies of photographic equipment ran out. Photographing stopped in 1943. These photos show prisoner number 26947. Her name was Katarzyna Kwoka and she was arrested as a political prisoner. She was brought to Auschwitz I on December 13, 1942, from Zamosc, Poland. She died on February 6, 1943.

Obedience

One of the most important lessons for **quarantine** prisoners was to obey any orders at once. Prisoners might have to stand in a day-long **roll call** or learn German marching songs or play leap-frog all day or do various exercises. Sometimes they spent the entire day taking their caps off and putting them on. Beatings were handed out all through the day. Tadeusz Sobolewicz remembers his first day in quarantine:

*The last of the work squads marched out through the main gate, while the rest went about their work in the camp. We still stood there, trying to keep warm. Then the **SS** men and the **blockältesters** came out and announced we had not taken our caps off the right way during roll call. So we had to lie on the ground, face down. As soon as we had done that we had to get up again.*

*And so on: "Get up! Lie down! Get up! Lie down!" over and over. The SS men and the **prisoner functionaries** were laughing together at this. But it was only the beginning. "Now, pay attention," said the blockältester. Now we had to hold our caps in our right hands and slap them against our right thighs, all at the same time. Of course, we couldn't. Those who had been too slow were pulled out of line, lined up against the wall, and questioned. The **Jews** and priest among them were repeatedly punched in the face, so that their heads then bounced off the wall. This sort of thing went on all day.*

Surviving Quarantine

This photo shows the quarantine camp at Mauthausen after **liberation.** In the background is the fence that separated the quarantine area from the rest of the camp.

Put to Work

These prisoners in Neuengamme **labor camp** have been taken from quarantine into the main camp and put to work.

Learning the Routine

Quarantine also got prisoners used to the camp routine. They got up at about 4 A.M. They had to make their beds neatly, use the toilets, wash, and dress as quickly as possible. They were then given breakfast and were rushed out to roll call. All through this, they had to move quickly, do things "properly," and obey orders in German. Any mistake, however small, meant a beating. For roll call they lined up in rows of ten because it made them easier to count. Roll call took place in the morning and evening. After the evening roll call the prisoners lined up for an evening meal. By 9 P.M. they were in their barracks and not allowed out until morning.

Part of the Camp

Once quarantine was over, the prisoners became part of the camp. They were moved out of the quarantine barracks, to make room for newcomers, and into ordinary barracks. Here they followed the same morning routines they had been taught, but they were put into work groups and worked from 6 A.M. to 5 P.M. with a half-hour meal break. This was the official work time. Many prisoners worked far longer.

Leon Greeman, an English Jew, was transferred to Auschwitz I and worked for a while unloading bricks: "You had four, six, or eight bricks loaded onto your shoulders and had to walk to a heap and unload them. The tops of my fingers were soon scraped raw."

The Main Camps

This map and list show the main camps in Greater Germany, a term used by the **Nazis** that included Germany, Austria, Czechoslovakia, and parts of Poland. The map and list do not include all of the sub-camps or any prisoner-of-war camps or holding camps. Nor do they show camps elsewhere in **occupied** Europe.

Camps in Greater Germany

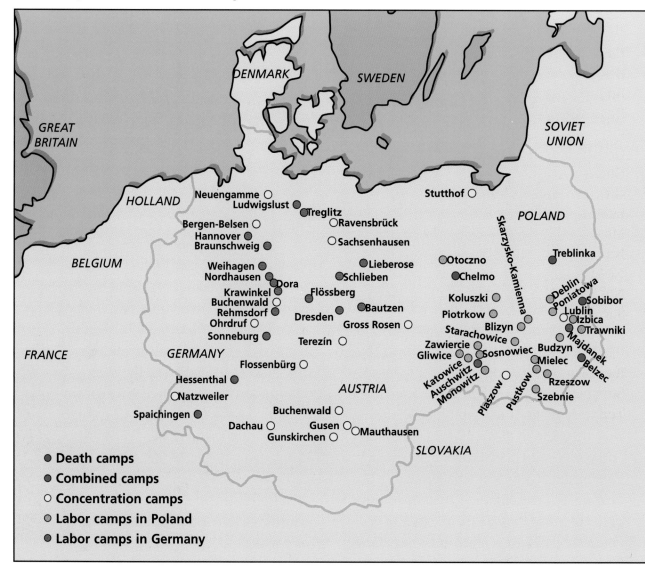

DENMARK
SWEDEN

GREAT
BRITAIN

SOVIET
UNION

HOLLAND

Neuengamme ○
Ludwigslust ○
Treglitz
Bergen-Belsen ○
Hannover ●
Braunschweig ●

Stutthof ○

POLAND

Skarzysko-Kamienna

○Ravensbrück
○ Sachsenhausen

Treblinka

BELGIUM

Weihagen ●
Nordhausen ●
Dora
Krawinkel ●
Buchenwald ○
Rehmsdorf ●
Ohrdruf ○
Sonneburg ●

●Lieberose
●Schlieben

Flössberg

○Otoczno
●Chelmo

Deblin
Poniatowa
Sobibor
Lublin
Izbica
Trawniki

Koluszki ○

●Bautzen

Dresden ●

Gross Rosen ○

Piotrkow ○

FRANCE

GERMANY

Terezín ○

Flossenbürg ○

Hessenthal ●
○Natzweiler

Spaichingen ●

AUSTRIA

Buchenwald ○

Dachau ○   Gusen ○
Gunskirchen ○ ○Mauthausen

Blizyn ○
Starachowice ●
Zawiercie ●
Gliwice ●   ●Sosnowiec
Katowice   ●
Auschwitz
Monowitz
Plaszow ○
Pustkow ○

Majdanek
Budzyn ●
Mielec ●
Belzec ●
Rzeszow ●
Szebnie ●

SLOVAKIA

- ● Death camps
- ● Combined camps
- ○ Concentration camps
- ◉ Labor camps in Poland
- ● Labor camps in Germany

Death camps

Belzec
Chelmno
Sobibor
Treblinka

Combined camps

Auschwitz-Birkenau
Majdanek

Concentration camps

Bergen-Belsen
Buchenwald
Dachau
Flossenbürg
Gross Rosen
Gunskirchen
Gusen
Lublin
Mauthausen
Natzweiler
Neuengamme
Novaky
Sachsenhausen
  [Oranienburg]
Plaszow
Ravensbrück
Stutthof
Terezín [Theresienstadt]

Labor camps and sub-camps in Poland

Blizyn
Bochnia
Budzyn
Czestochowa
Deblin
Gliwice
Izbica
Katowice
Koluszki
Mielec
Monowitz
Otoczno
Piotrkow
Poniatowa
Pustkow
Rzeszow
Skarzysko-Kamienna
Sosnowiec
Szebnie
Trawniki
Zawiercie

Labor camps in Germany

Bautzen
Braunschweig
Dora
Dresden
Flössberg
Hannover
Hessenthal
Krawinkel
Lieberose
Ludwigslust
Nordhausen
Rehmsdorf
Schlieben
Sonneberg
Spaichingen
Treglitz
Wiehagen

Majdanek

An aerial view of Majdanek **concentration** and **death camp** taken by the **Allies** during the war.

Timeline

1933

January 30	The **Nazi** Party comes to power in Germany. Adolf Hitler, their leader, is elected Chancellor. Membership in the **SS** reaches more than 50,000.
February 27	A fire breaks out at the *Reichstag,* the German parliament.
February 28	German President Hindenburg's decree, "For the Protection of the People and the State," allows for the creation of **concentration camps.** The Nazis persuade Hindenburg to pass the decree to fight what they call the "**Communist** threat."
March 21	Dachau, the first Nazi concentration camp, is set up. Concentration camps and **labor camps** are set up steadily after this.
May 2	Trade unions are banned in Germany.
July 14	**Political** parties other than the Nazi Party are banned in Germany.

1934

July 20	The SS is no longer under the control of the German army.
August 2	Hitler makes himself *Führer,* sole leader of Germany.

1936

March 29	The SS grows to 3,500 men.
June 17	Himmler is placed in charge of all police departments.

1937

July 16	Buchenwald concentration camp is set up.

1938

March 13	Germany takes over Austria.
August 8	Mauthausen concentration camp is set up.
November 9	*Kristallnacht* takes place. Nazi-led violence against **Jews** includes burning synagogues and looting Jewish stores and homes.

1939

September 1	Germany invades Poland. Nazis begin to pass laws against Polish Jews restricting the work they can do, as in Germany in 1933–1936.
September 3	Britain and France declare war on Germany.
September 17	The Soviet Union invades Poland from the east.
September 28	Germany and the Soviet Union split Poland up between them.

1940

February 12	The first Jews are deported from Germany to **ghettos** in Poland.
April 9	Germany invades Denmark and Norway.
April 27	Himmler builds a camp at Auschwitz.
April 30	A large ghetto is set up in the Polish city of Lodz. All Jews from the city and the surrounding area are sent there. More ghettos are planned in other Polish cities for Polish Jews, and then for Jews from other lands controlled by Germany.
May 10	Germany invades Belgium, France, Luxembourg, and Holland.

1941

April 6	Germany invades Yugoslavia and Greece.
June 22	Germany invades the Soviet Union and begins killing Jews in large numbers as the German army moves through the Soviet Union.
June 25	Finland declares war on Russia and so becomes an ally of Germany.
September 1	All German Jews over the age of six have to wear a yellow Star of David with "*Jude*" written in black on it.
From September	Mass gassings at Auschwitz begin with Soviet prisoners-of-war and continue. They focus on Jews and become more regular from January 1942.
October 16	Mass deportation of Jews to Poland begins.
October 28	10,000 Jews are selected and killed at Kovno Ghetto in Lithuania.
December 7	Japan bombs Pearl Harbor.
December 8	The first group of Jews are gassed at Chelmno **death camp** in Poland.
December 11	Germany declares war on the United States.

1942

January 20	The Wannsee Conference is called to discuss the "Final Solution" to the "Jewish Problem."
March 1	The first deportation of Jews to Sobibor death camp in Poland takes place.
March 17	The first deportation of Jews to Belzec death camp in Poland takes place.
March 26	The first deportations to Auschwitz-Birkenau and Majdanek death camps take place.
March 27	The first deportation of French Jews to Auschwitz takes place.
July 15	The first group of Dutch Jews are deported to Auschwitz.
July 22	Daily deportations to Treblinka camp in Poland from the Warsaw Ghetto begin.
October 4	Himmler orders that all Jews in concentration camps are to be sent to Auschwitz-Birkenau to be killed.

1943

June 11	Himmler orders all remaining ghettos to be emptied and their inhabitants killed.

1944

March 23	The deportation of Greek Jews begins.
April 7	Two Jews escape from Auschwitz and reach Brostalvia in Slovakia. News of the camp can no longer be ignored in the west.
May 15	Mass deportation and gassing of Hungarian Jews begins.
From June	Death marches from camps in Poland begin. Prisoners are marched westward, in front of advancing Soviet troops.
June 6	**Allied** troops land in Normandy, France.

1945

January 17	The final death march from Auschwitz-Birkenau takes place.
January 27	Soviet troops reach Auschwitz.
April 11	U.S. troops reach Buchenwald camp.
April 15	British troops reach Belsen camp.
April 29	U.S. troops reach Dachau camp. Russian troops reach Berlin camp.
April 30	Hitler commits suicide in Berlin.
May 5	U.S. troops reach Mauthausen camp.
May 7	Germany surrenders to the Allies.
November 20	The Nuremberg trials of Nazi war criminals begin. The first war criminals are executed in October 1946.

Glossary

Ally country that fought against Nazi Germany in World War II

Aryan word used by the Nazis to mean people with northern European ancestors, without any ancestors from what they called "inferior" races, such as Poles, Slavs, or Jews. Aryans were usually blonde, blue-eyed, and sturdy.

asocial Nazi term for people who did not support the Nazi state. Asocials could be drunks, people who would not work, homosexuals, or members of a religious group whose beliefs might make them oppose the Nazis.

authorization written permission to do something from someone in power

blockältester prisoner put in charge of a barracks; women were called *blockälteste*

cholera disease that causes vomiting and diarrhea. It is caused by dirty conditions and is spread by water polluted with sewage. Cholera can be fatal.

citizen person who belongs to a country and who has rights in that country, such as protection by the law, and duties to that country, such as paying taxes

commandant person in charge of a camp

Communist person who believes that a country should be governed by the people of that country for the good of everyone in it. They believe private property is wrong, including owning a home or a business. The state should own everything and run everything, giving the people the things they need.

concentration camp prison camp set up by the Nazis under a special law that meant that the prisoners were never tried and were never given a release date. The Nazis could put anyone in these camps, for any reason or none, for as long as they wanted.

crematorium place with special ovens for burning bodies

death camp camp set up by the Nazis to murder as many people, most of them Jewish, as quickly and cheaply as possible. Most of the victims were gassed.

Einsatzkommando special units of the German army set up by the Nazis. These units went into eastern Europe at the same time as the army. Their job was supposedly to round up and kill civilians who were a danger to the Reich. In fact, they were told to kill Jews.

frostbite infection of the skin caused by extreme cold. Untreated frostbite can cause gangrene, which makes the affected part of the body rot away.

gas chamber large room, often disguised as showers, that the Nazis filled with people. When the room was full, the Nazis pumped gas into it to kill the people inside.

Gestapo secret police set up by the Nazis in 1933

ghetto area of a town or city, walled or fenced off from the rest of the city, where Jewish people were forced to live

Holocaust huge destruction or sacrifice. When it appears with a capital "H," it refers to the deliberate attempt by the Nazi government in Germany to destroy all of the Jewish people in their power.

informer person who tells one group of people what their opponents are planning

Jehovah's Witnesses religious group that was especially persecuted by the Nazis because members refused to swear an oath of loyalty to Hitler

Jew (Jewish) someone who follows the Jewish faith. The Nazis also called people Jews if they had Jewish ancestors, even if they had changed their faith.

Judenfrei "Jew Free;" a place with no Jewish people living there

kapo prisoner who is put in charge of other prisoners when they are working

labor camp camp set up by the Nazis that was a prison that used the prisoners as cheap labor

liberated used in this book to mean a place, especially a concentration camp, being freed from the control of the SS. Camps were liberated by Allied soldiers.

Nazi member of the Nazi Party. Nazi is short for *Nationalsozialistische Deutsche Arbeiterpartei*, the National Socialist German Workers' Party.

occupied used in this book to mean a country that has been captured by Germany and is ruled by Nazis supported by the German army

political having to do with ideas and actions of government; person arrested for opposing Nazi ideas or actions

prisoner functionary prisoner, usually a German criminal, put in charge of other prisoners as a *kapo* or *blockältester*

propaganda information and ideas that are worded and presented so that people will accept and believe them, even if they are not true

protective custody arrest under the law, "For the Protection of the People and the State," passed in February 1933, that allowed the German police to arrest people for as long as they like without bringing them to trial

quarantine to keep people who might be carrying a disease away from other people so they will not spread that disease. Used by the Nazis to refer to the first few days or weeks people spent in a new camp. The Nazis said the quarantine was medical, but it was really to terrorize the prisoners into obedience.

race group of people with the same ancestors

Reich empire. *See* Third Reich.

Reichmark (RM) German money under the Nazis

resettle to take people away from one place and make them settle somewhere else. Jewish people who were moved to the ghettos and then to the camps by the Nazis were promised they would be "resettled" in the east.

roll call count of all prisoners in a camp, usually morning and evening

SS (short for *Schutzstaffel*) security staff. The SS began as Hitler's personal bodyguard. Later, they ran concentration camps and death camps. Everyone in the SS swore loyalty to Hitler, rather than Germany.

selection used in this book to refer to the SS process in the camps of choosing which people to kill

Third Reich "the third empire." The Nazis saw their rule as the third German empire, with Hitler as the emperor, or *Führer*.

transport used in this book to refer to a trainload of people being sent to the camps

typhus disease caused by dirty conditions and spread by polluted water, usually polluted with sewage. Typhus causes high temperatures, rashes, vomiting, and diarrhea. It can be fatal.

undesirable word used by the Nazis to describe any person that they did not approve of because of political beliefs, race, religion, or behavior

Further Reading

Frank, Anne. *Diary of a Young Girl.* Columbus, Ohio: Prentice Hall, 1993.

Shuter, Jane. *Auschwitz.* Chicago: Heinemann Library, 1999.

Tames, Richard. *Anne Frank.* Chicago: Heinemann Library, 1998.

Tames, Richard. *Adolf Hitler.* Chicago: Heinemann Library, 1998.

Whittock, Martyn. *Hitler & National Socialism.* Chicago: Heinemann Library, 1996.

Wiesel, Elie. *Night.* New York: Bantam Books, 1982.

Willoughby, Susan. *The Holocaust.* Chicago: Heinemann Library, 2000.

Sources

The author and publisher gratefully acknowledge the publications from which written sources in this book are drawn. In some cases, the wording or sentence structure has been simplified to make the material appropriate for a school readership.

Beon, Yves. *Planet Dora*: *A Memoir of the Holocaust and the Birth of the Space Age.* Boulder, Colo.: Westview Press, 1997. (pp. 20, 24)

Bresheeth, Haim, Stuart Hood, and Litza Jansz. *The Holocaust for Beginners.* Cambridge, UK: Icon Books, 1994. (p. 19)

Dwork, Deborah and Robert Jan van Pelt. *Auschwitz: 1270 to Present.* Scranton, Penn.: W. W. Norton & Company, 1996. (pp. 7, 13)

Gibbon, Constantine Fritz and Krystyna Michalik (translators). *KL Auschwitz Seen By the SS.* Oswiecim, Poland: Auschwitz-Birkenau State Museum, 1998. (pp. 10, 14, 16, 21–22, 27–28, 32, 34, 36)

Gilbert, Martin. *The Boys*: *The Story of 732 Young Concentration Camp Survivors.* New York: Henry Holt & Company, 1997. (p. 42)

Gryn, Hugo. *Chasing Shadows.* East Rutherford, N.J.: Viking Penguin, 2000. (pp. 25, 26, 41, 43)

Klee, Ernst, Willi Dressen, and Volker Riess (editors). *The Good Old Days: The Holocaust as Seen By Its Perpetrators and Bystanders.* Old Saybrook, Conn.: William S. Konecky Associates, Inc., 1997. (pp. 19, 23, 24, 32)

"The Nazi State: Machine or Morass." *History Today.* London: History Today Ltd., 1986. (pp. 9, 32)

Noakes, J. and G. Pridham. *Nazism, 1919-1945.* Exeter, UK: University of Exeter Press, 1991. (pp. 4, 9, 15, 30, 37)

Rees, Laurence. *The Nazis: A Warning from History.* New York: The New Press, 1997. (p. 35)

Selvage, Douglas (translator). *Auschwitz: Nazi Death Camp.* Oswiecim, Poland: Auschwitz-Birkenau State Museum, 1998. (pp. 20, 40)

Sobolewicz, Tadeusz. *But I Survived.* Oswiecim, Poland: Auschwitz-Birkenau State Museum, 1998. (pp. 25, 44, 46)

Places of Interest and Websites

C.A.N.D.L.E.S. Holocaust Museum (Children of Auschwitz Nazi Deadly Labs Experiments)
1532 South Third Street
Terre Haute, IN 47802
Visitor information: (812) 234-7881
Website: *http://www.candles-museum.org*

Museum of Jewish Heritage: A Living Memorial to the Holocaust
18 First Place
Battery Park City
New York, NY 10004
Visitor information: (212) 509-6130
Website: *http://www.mjhnyc.org*

Simon Wiesenthal Center: Museum of Tolerance
Simon Wiesenthal Plaza
9736 West Pico Blvd.
Los Angeles, CA 90035
Visitor information: (310) 553-8403
Website: *http://www.museumoftolerance.com*

St. Louis Holocaust Museum and Learning Center
12 Millstone Campus Drive
St. Louis, MO 63146
Visitor information: (314) 432-0020
Website: *http://www.hmlc.org*

United States Holocaust Memorial Museum
100 Raoul Wallenberg Place, SW
Washington, D.C. 20024
Visitor information: (202) 488-0400
Website: *http://www.ushmm.org*

Website warning
1. Almost all Holocaust websites have been designed for adult users. They can contain horrifying and upsetting information and pictures.
2. Some people wish to minimize the Holocaust, or even deny that it happened at all. Some of their websites pretend to be delivering unbiased facts and information. To be sure you are getting accurate information, it is always best to use an officially recognized site such as the ones listed on this page.
3. If you plan to visit a Holocaust website, ask an adult to view the site with you.

Index